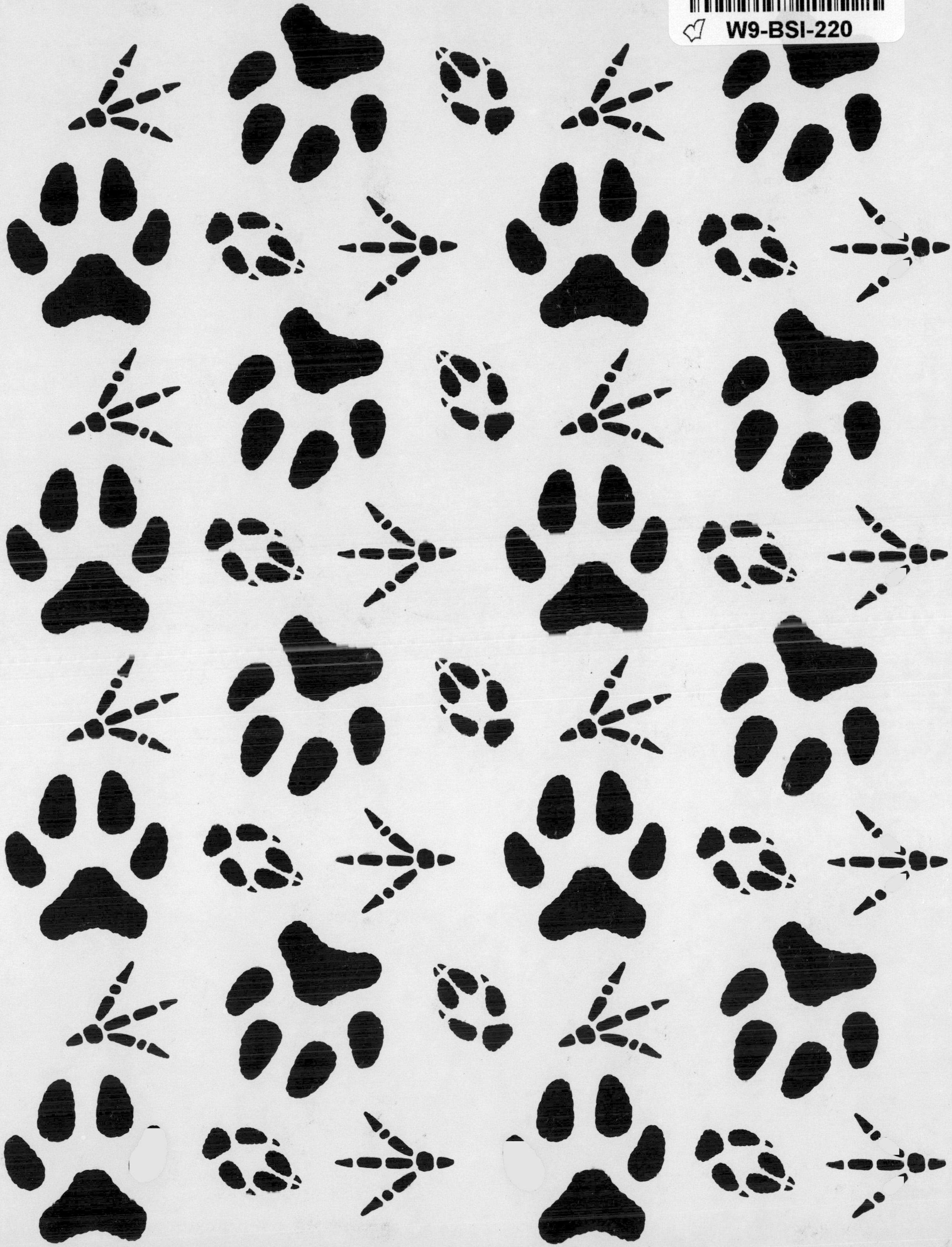

A DK PUBLISHING BOOK

Written and edited by
David Nicoll and Jane Donnelly
Art Editor Mandy Earey
Deputy Managing Editor Dawn Sirett
Deputy Managing Art Editor
C. David Gillingwater
US Editor Camela Decaire
Production Katy Holmes
Picture Research Christine Rista
Photography Peter Anderson, Geoff Brightling,
Frank Greenaway, Dave King, Jerry Young
Illustrators Ellis Nadler and
Derek Matthews
Consultant Juliet Clutton-Brock

First American Edition, 1996
2 4 6 8 10 9 7 5 3 1

Published in the United States by DK Publishing, Inc.,
95 Madison Avenue, New York, New York 10016
Visit us on the World Wide Web at http://www.dk.com

A CIP catalog record is available from the Library of Congress.

ISBN: 0-7894-1111-3

Color reproduction by Chromagraphics, Singapore
Printed and bound in Italy by L.E.G.O.

DK would like to thank the following for their kind
permission to reproduce photographs:
t=top, b=bottom, c=center, l=left, r=right
Bruce Coleman / Peter Davey 6tl; Johnny Johnson 15cr;
Wayne Lankinen 12bc; Mike McKavett 9tl; Jim Simmen 15bl,
Rod Williams 19tr; **Planet Earth Pictures** / James D. Watt 20bl;
Tony Stone Images 8tl, 8bl, 9cr; **Zefa** 10bl, 11cr, 18tl, 18bl, 21tr.

Scale
Look for drawings like
this – they show the size of the
animals compared with people.

Tiger

Cheetah

Gray wolf

Alligator

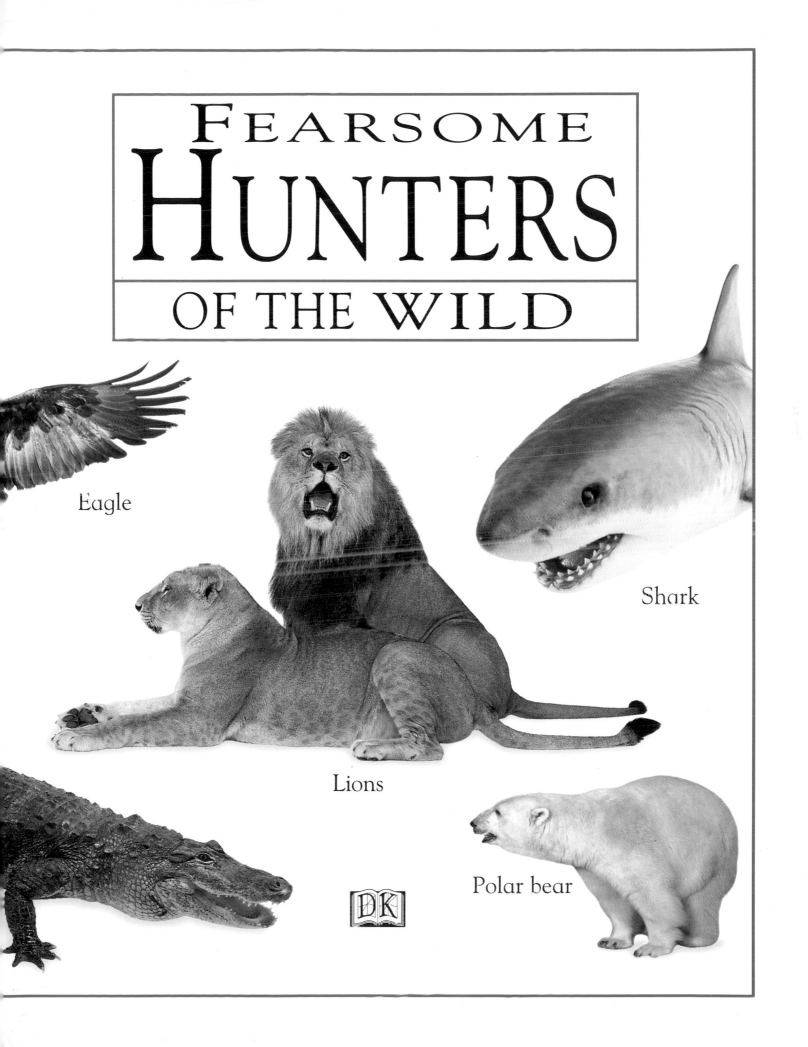

FEARSOME HUNTERS
OF THE WILD

Eagle

Shark

Lions

Polar bear

Lion

AMAZING FACTS

🐾 An adult male lion weighs about 440 lb (200 kg) – that's more than two grown men.

🐾 Lions are the only big cats that live in family groups.

🐾 Although females do most of the hunting, male lions get to eat first at a kill.

Claws are pulled in when not needed.

Fearsome fangs, cutting claws, and a powerful, muscular body make the lion the mighty king of the carnivores. Today these big cats are found only on the grasslands of Africa and in a small part of India.

Lions have good eyesight and can see clearly in the dark.

Lionesses do not have manes.

Lady killers
Female lions, called lionesses, are smaller than male lions. They do most of the hunting, killing zebras, antelopes, and other animals.

 Animals that eat only other animals are called **carnivores**.

Large, heavy paws

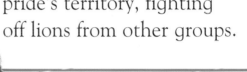

A male lion's mane makes him look big and scary.

Pride protectors
Male lions defend their pride's territory, fighting off lions from other groups.

Scale

Pale golden fur blends in with the scorched African grasslands, providing a perfect disguise.

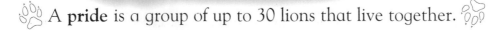

A **pride** is a group of up to 30 lions that live together.

Alligator

AMAGING FACTS

AMAZING FACTS

Baby alligators grow so quickly during their first year they almost double in size.

Most alligators live for about 50 years, but some have been known to live for more than 100 years!

An alligator's bellow is as loud as a noisy engine. Alligators make this noise to communicate with each other.

This American alligator lurks in rivers in the southeastern United States. It drags large prey underwater and rolls over and over as it bites off the victim's flesh with its deadly gripping jaws.

Cruise control
Alligators swim fast. Their powerful tails silently push and steer them through water.

Webbed feet

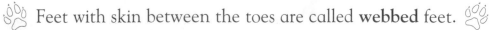

Feet with skin between the toes are called **webbed** feet.

Crocodile cousins

Crocodiles and alligators look a lot alike, but you can tell them apart! When its mouth is closed, an alligator's teeth are hidden, but the fourth tooth on a crocodile's lower jaw sticks out when its mouth is shut.

Stone supper

Alligators and crocodiles swallow stones. This helps their stomachs grind up food, which they swallow whole.

Crocodile's prominent tooth

Tough scales

Scale

Eager eater

When young, alligators feed on small fish, frogs, and toads, swallowing them whole. Fully grown, they catch larger prey. They hide underwater with just their eyes and nose above the surface, waiting to attack.

Scales are waterproof plates that some animals have on their skin.

Cheetah

The cheetah is the fastest land animal in the world. Its wiry, streamlined body and powerful leg muscles allow it to run at about 60 mph (100 km/h) over short distances.

Scale

Speeding hunter
Cheetahs can hunt even fast-running animals, such as antelopes and gazelles. They stalk their prey, then launch after it at top speed, killing it with a bite to the neck.

Long whiskers help a cheetah judge its distance from its prey.

Caring for cubs
A mother cheetah may have up to eight cubs in one litter. Like all cats, the cubs are born blind and helpless and the mother takes care of them for at least a year.

The cheetah is the only cat whose claws are permanently extended, giving extra grip on the ground.

A group of baby animals born at the same time to one mother is called a **litter**.

Golden eyes

Cheetahs usually hunt at dawn or dusk. Their huge amber eyes help them spot prey on the grasslands of Africa and southwestern Asia.

Yellow fur dappled with black markings camouflages a cheetah as it watches and waits for prey.

When turning sharply, a cheetah uses its long, flicking tail to balance.

🐾 A cheetah is so powerful that it can accelerate faster than a sports car – so don't ever bother to race one!

🐾 A cheetah's long legs and flexible backbone allow it to take such big strides that it looks as if it is flying through the air.

🐾 A cheetah's tail is very long. It's more than half the length of the cheetah's body.

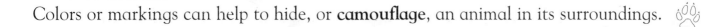

Colors or markings can help to hide, or **camouflage**, an animal in its surroundings. 🐾

Polar bear

Polar bears are the mighty meat eaters of the Arctic. They use their swiping paws and sharp teeth to kill seals – their main source of food.

Fat, called blubber, lies under the fur to keep the bear warm.

Deep-freeze living

With their warm fur coats and thick layers of fat, polar bears can live in temperatures nearly ten times colder than a refrigerator.

Patience pays

To get a good meal, a polar bear must wait by a breathing hole for a seal to appear from under the ice. A bear may not eat for five days, traveling from hole to hole.

Seals breathe air through holes in the ice called **breathing holes**.

Thick, water-repellent fur insulates the bear in freezing Arctic conditions.

Scale

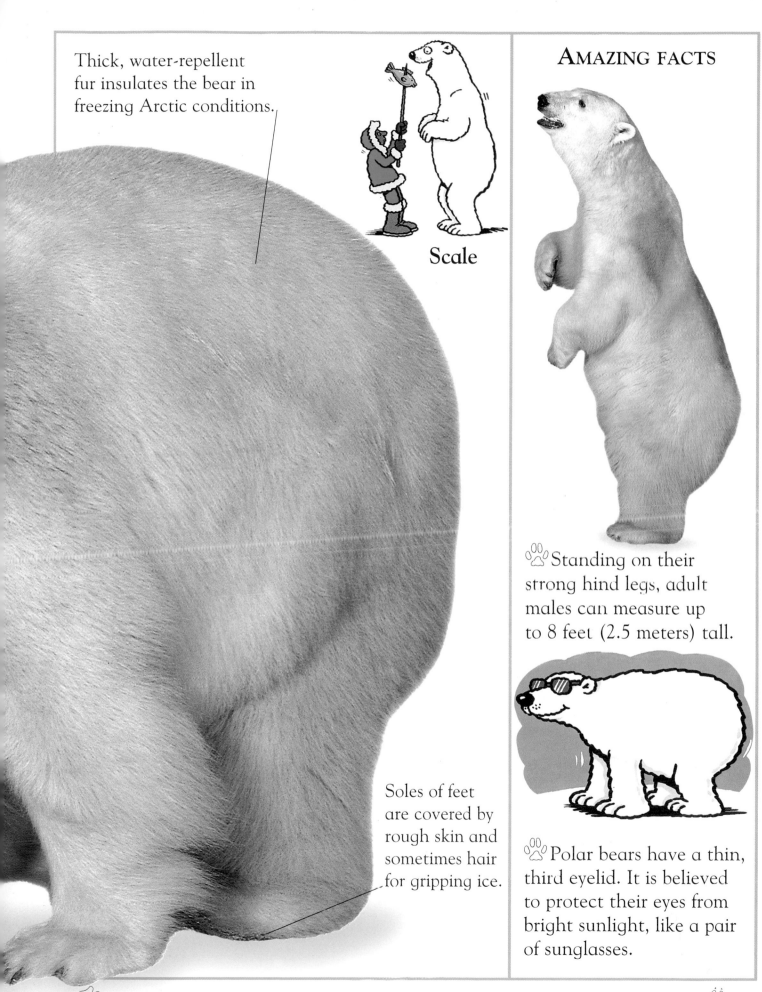

🐾 Standing on their strong hind legs, adult males can measure up to 8 feet (2.5 meters) tall.

Soles of feet are covered by rough skin and sometimes hair for gripping ice.

🐾 Polar bears have a thin, third eyelid. It is believed to protect their eyes from bright sunlight, like a pair of sunglasses.

🐾 Something that **insulates** protects, in this case by keeping out cold and water. 🐾

Eagle

Excellent eyesight, huge talons, and tearing beaks make eagles powerful birds of prey. Diving at speeds up to 100 mph (160 km/h), golden eagles suddenly swoop down to grab birds, hares, and other small mammals.

Scale

Tips of feathers push and steer an eagle through the air.

A **talon** is a sharp, hooked claw.

The golden eagle's wingspan measures more than 6 feet (2 meters) across.

Eagles flap their wings with deep, strong strokes.

AMAZING FACTS

Spread out, an eagle's wings and tail feathers act like brakes in midair.

Bald eagles mate for life and often return to the same nests each year.

Eagle eyes

Imagine seeing four times better than you can now. That's how well eagles see. This bald eagle can spy a fish 3 mi (5 km) away as a distant speck in the water.

Mostly made of sticks, aeries can weigh more than 2.2 tons (2 tonnes) – that's as heavy as two minivans.

 An **aerie** is an eagle's nest.

Wild dogs

Dingo

Dingos live wild in the remote, dry desert areas of Australia, called the outback. They hunt prey such as lizards, rabbits, and wallabies and also scavenge in towns for scraps.

Scale

African wild dog

Packs of African wild dogs chase prey such as antelopes on the African grasslands. They can reach speeds of up to 30 mph (50 km/h). After a hunt, adult dogs take food to the pups. They chew and swallow pieces of meat, then regurgitate the remains to feed their young.

Scale

Long, muscular legs allow for fast running.

Wolves and most wild dogs live and hunt in family groups called **packs.**

Gray wolf

Wolves are the largest members of the dog family at heights up to 3 ft (1 m). Like all dogs, they have well-developed senses to help them hunt a variety of prey, including deer, rabbits, and snakes.

Scale

A wolf has 42 teeth in its powerful jaws.

Strong legs can carry a wolf at speeds of up to 40 mph (65 km/h) in short bursts.

To **regurgitate** is to bring up partially digested food from the stomach.

Tiger

At more than 10 feet (3 meters) from nose to tail, a fully grown tiger is a magnificent sight. A stealthy, solitary hunter, the tiger silently stalks its prey with awesome power and grace.

🐾 Unlike most cats, tigers are excellent swimmers and often lie in water during the day to keep cool.

🐾 Tigers can make huge single leaps – they could even reach the height of a bus in one jump.

Powerful hunter

Tigers can bring down large prey such as cattle. They swallow big chunks of meat and can break through bone with one crunch of their strong jaws.

🐾 Tigers are hard to see. Their fur blends in with the jungle vegetation.

Paws are so strong they can knock over prey with one mighty blow.

🐾 A **jungle** is a tropical rain forest. **Vegetation** is another word for plants. 🐾

Cool cat

The largest tigers live in snowy Siberia. There are now only about 200 tigers living in this area. The rest live in other parts of Asia. All tigers are endangered – there may be less than 5,000 left altogether.

Siberian tigers have thicker fur than Indian tigers.

The tiger is the biggest and heaviest cat. Indian tigers can weigh up to 450 lb (260 kg).

A tiger keeps its claws pulled in until it needs them for cutting and slashing.

Scale

Endangered animals are dying out and soon may not exist.

Shark

AMAZING FACTS

🐾 The harmless whale shark is the largest fish at nearly 40 feet (12 meters) long. If it could stand on its tail it would be four stories high.

🐾 Hammerhead sharks usually swim in schools. Their eyes are on either side of their wide heads.

🐾 Special sensors along their sides help sharks detect movements of prey.

There are many species of sharks living in oceans around the world. Most are harmless to people, but a few are extremely dangerous. This great white shark is the largest and most deadly hunting shark. Its diet ranges from fish to seals.

Pelvic fin acts like a stabilizer, stopping the shark from rolling over as it swims.

The shark is pushed through the water by its tail, and, when hunting prey, it can reach speeds of up to 15 mph (25 km/h).

Scale

🐾 A group of sharks swimming together is called a **school**. 🐾

Dental wealth

When a great white's front teeth wear down, another row moves forward to replace them. There's plenty of room for all these teeth – one of the largest sets of great white jaws ever found was 22.5 in (57.5 cm) wide.

A third eyelid protects the eye when the shark attacks its prey.

Gill slits

The teeth of a great white shark are about 1.5 in (4 cm) long.

A shark breathes underwater through its **gills,** which absorb oxygen from water.

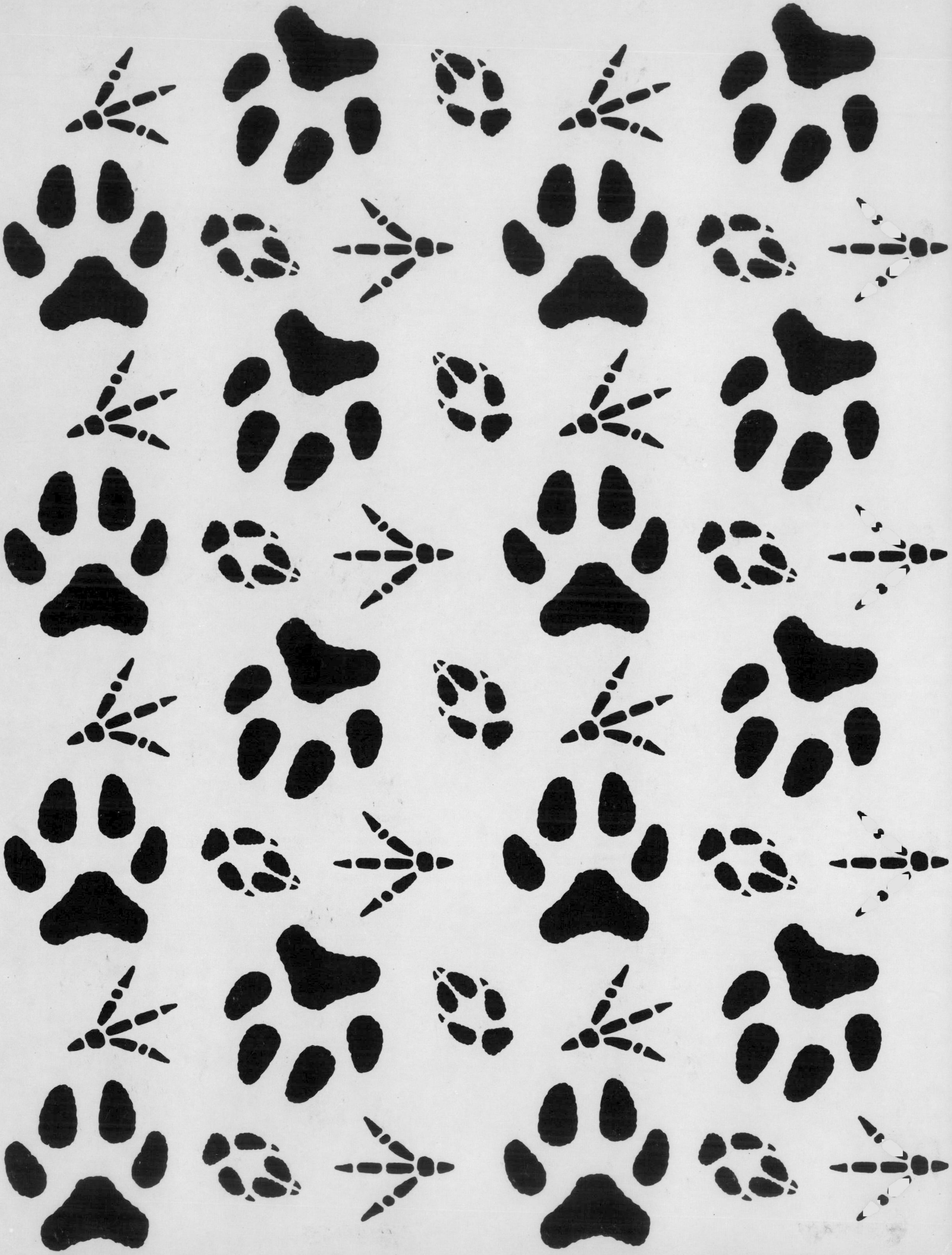